FIRING UP YOUR
POWERPOINT

10
Immutable Laws for Presenting in the Digital Era

LEE FEATHERBY

Copyright © 2021 by Lee Featherby

All rights reserved. No part of this publication may be reproduced, distributed, or transmitted in any form or by any means, including photocopying, recording, or other electronic or mechanical methods, without the prior written permission of the publisher, except in the case of brief quotations embodied in critical reviews and certain other noncommercial uses permitted by copyright law.

For permission request, write to the publisher addressed "Attention: Permissions Coordinator," at lee@mrpresentations.me

Print ISBN: 978-0-646-83623-2

E-book ISBN: 978-0-646-83624-9

Cover and Book Design by PowerfulPoints.

Printing and Publishing by The Big Smoke Media Group.

First printing edition 2021.

About the Author

I was first exposed to presentations in the early 80s while working for Cadbury-Schweppes. I was mesmerised when I delivered a presentation using nine slide projectors, driven by a reel-to-reel tape deck. At that time, it was state-of-the-art and little did I know my life would ultimately be dedicated to perfecting the art of creating effective presentations.

That presentation took two graphic designers and the manager of the Marketing Services Division about three months to create. The same thing could be done today by one designer in a month, such are the improvements to the technology.

From the time I started using PowerPoint in 1997, I became a devotee. The unique thing about PowerPoint is that many think that simply learning to use the software is the same as learning how to build and craft a good presentation. This is like saying learning Word makes you a good writer. As a result, many blame the rise of bad presentations on PowerPoint.

PowerfulPoints was started in 2003, after helping my then-partner put together a lecture entitled The Pathophysiology of the Gastrointestinal Tract. She said I was good at it, and I should do it as a business. I looked around and couldn't find anyone in Australia who was doing it, so I set up a website, got a few clients, and the business has taken on a life of its own. In fact, I remember saying at the time, I can't ever see it doing more than $10,000 per month in sales.

I now have about 19 staff and offices in Shanghai and Sydney, and count some of the world's biggest brands as clients. I have also had the opportunity to train people across continents in some of the world's largest brands. Maybe I'm no good at business forecasting, but make up for it by knowing a few things about creating effective presentations.

With the advent of COVID-19, the world of presenting took an unforeseen turn and suddenly people were forced to deliver via camera while others watched on a screen. This in effect magnified the failings of our presentation creation skills, as now the audience could very easily turn to emails, phone calls and other distractions during a presentation, so engaging the audience and delivering your message became even harder.

In fact, research we undertook in December 2020 showed that 75% read emails, 41% took phone calls, 30% went to the toilet and 7% even admitted resting their eyes or going to sleep during a virtual presentation!

I have long been of the belief that the world doesn't need another book on presentations; there are already some great — and not so great — books out there. But I've been asked to write a book specifically on the subject with a focus on the new challenges of the digital/virtual presentation.

I have tried to keep it brief, as you're likely time-poor, and my philosophy around communication has always been to keep it sharp and to the point. You're reading this to get better at what you do, so let's get to it.

Most of my ideas are backed by science, some by personal experience. In most cases, I have omitted my references, preferring to just give you the details. Should you like further evidence backing up what I am saying, feel free to get in contact.

Being able to share my knowledge is always a privilege. I always enjoy hearing your feedback, comments, and contributions. Please enjoy, and make the most of this expertise to make your presentations more engaging and effective.

Contents

Introduction: Communication Has Changed, Presentations Haven't	11
One: Set a Clear Outcome	17
Two: Content is King, Structure is Queen	21
Three: It's All About the Why	23
Four: Slides Support Your Talk	29
Five: Make Your Proposition, Then Prove It	31
Six: Use Your Titles to Deliver Your Key Messages and Tell Your Story	33
Seven: Be Animated	39
Eight: Start Big, Become Small	43
Nine: Keep Slide Content to a Minimum	47
Ten: No Third Level Bullet Points	51
And now...	53
Acknowledgments	55

INTRODUCTION

Communication Has Changed, Presentations Haven't

If you look at presentations and compare them from, say, 1997 to today, they haven't changed much: most presentations are text-heavy and data-heavy.

They haven't changed in a world that has massively changed in terms of visual communications. Compared to 1997, technology and the means for communicating are almost unrecognisable: we have digital phones, we have broadband Internet, social media, streaming media, all sorts of ways in which we communicate and have messages delivered to us. Even outdoor advertising has changed significantly in style and technology compared to how it was at the end of the 20th century.

These days however, we are even more challenged, as very often we need to present this material through a camera, onto a screen, sometimes a small 13" laptop screen and more rarely, a phone screen. In case you've never done it, a camera doesn't give you the feedback a live audience does. In some cases, you may get to see the audience, very often you don't, so it's hard to gauge their engagement.

For the audience, they don't get the eye contact of a normal presentation, and eye contact is a critical factor in effective and engaging communication.

Another significant impact stems from the number of messages we are exposed to each day. Think about the often-unnoticed messaging in Facebook or the tweets you receive. Then, compare the quality of these messages to what most people try and deliver in a presentation, either online or in person.

The fact is many presentations are still text- and data-heavy. When we start giving these text- and data-heavy presentations, the audience just switches off! We all know this but persist in giving them. Why? Because we don't know what else to do. Well, this book will hopefully help!

The problem is not PowerPoint

In some research done by Ken Davis for his book Secrets of Dynamic Communication, more than 70% of people leaving a presentation had no idea what was being communicated. As Ken points out, that isn't even the sad statistic. More than 50% of THE SPEAKERS couldn't tell you what the objective of the presentation was! Our own research in December 2020 didn't back this up (it came in at 11%), but I won't challenge his numbers.

People aren't trained in how to create presentations and they confuse knowing the software with knowing how to build an effective presentation. Most learn the craft from one of several areas, depending on their age: learnt at school, learnt at university, learnt from their boss, or just did what was expected when they got the job.

All these processes embed bad habits, as poor presentation technique gets perpetuated. The result is the situation we have today.

The blame lies squarely on industry and academia. I used to lecture at several universities and they did nothing to upskill their staff in better pedagogical techniques like effective presenting. Nor have many recognised communications, and presentations alike, as a vital management skill and mandated it as part of their undergraduate or postgraduate programs.

So too, industry tends to complain about poor presentation skills by its employees and sends them on a course to improve, but those courses just teach them delivery techniques with scant regard given to constructing powerful presentations in the first place.

To be successful, you need to make it easy

To be successful these days, you need to understand the context through which presentations are seen in the 21st century, whether they be in person or digitally.

Recently, COVID-19 changed everything. People spend more time staring at a computer screen than they do in real time meetings. People are busy; busier than they have been in the past. I am old enough, unfortunately, to have been around when PCs first came out. All the futurists were saying that the development of the PC will give us more leisure time. I have less leisure time now than I ever had in the past!

The technology has fundamentally facilitated a shift in the average number of direct reports a manager has. In the 1960s, it was six reports per manager. The modern-day average is 12, a factor facilitated using computers and other technology. These days, most people go from meeting, to meeting, to meeting, to meeting; they no longer have the opportunity to sit back and reflect on what was said in each, and this impacts the way we need to deliver presentations.

So, what does this mean?

What happens when we're asked to do a presentation? Usually, we put it in the drawer and wait two or three days before the event, then think "Oh my, I have to do that presentation." You pull it out, start looking through past presentations and ask colleagues to find any slides that might somehow be useful.

We start to pull things together. But we start that presentation in the context of what we want to tell them. But a good presentation needs to put it from the point of view of what they need to know in order to make the decision we want them to make. This is a different approach; it's what I call an audience-focused approach to presentations.

It might be a presentation to your Board of Management, or your executive leadership team. It might be a new product launch; it might be an IPO. There are any number of reasons to present, including just to update people on a situation, but turning the 'it' from what you want to say to what they need to know is a critical factor in developing a powerful presentation.

A presentation needs to tell them what they want to know, or what they need to know, to make the decision that I might be wanting them to make. This is the most significant aspect of making presentations in the digital world: it's not about what you want to say, it's about what they need to know!

Make the information easy to find

The second thing you need to do is make sure the key messages are clear and easy to find.

It amazes me that people become so focused on the information, they forget the reason they are presenting: to give people information, very often so they can make informed decision making and yet they end up doing exactly the opposite. One thing we are not short of today is information. What is critical then, is to identify the relevant information and understand what that means: what is the key message being delivered from it. More than ever we need to identify what's important, what's relevant and what's not and build a presentation accordingly.

Years ago, I was looking at a sales deck on behalf of a prospective client. It was in the early stages of voice recognition on telephones, and this company's product resulted in an 11% reduction in misdirected calls.

This was an English company with 42 million calls a year, resulting in 4 million calls that no longer went to the wrong place. That amazing statistic was buried in ten-point type, somewhere in the middle of the slide.

It's such a big selling point to say "4 million calls will end up going to the right person," and yet it was put right in the middle of the deck.

Too often, we need to be much clearer about what our key messages are, and make sure that we make them easy for the audience to find.

It's not a data dump

The big buzzword about business now is 'story'. But what does that mean? What does it mean to make a story? Does that mean wrapping the presentation up around a saga about going sailing somewhere?

No. It means you need to have a conversation with people. We have conversations with people every day but we don't tend to put our presentations in the same context; they're not different. When you have a conversation with someone, you don't just dump information, delivering them one fact after another. You tell a story or make an argument for something… which is basically the same thing as a story.

You need to make sure that you take your audience on a journey, rather than just dumping information. There's nothing more boring than looking at data slide after data slide that's not relevant. To bring about change in someone requires effort. You need to make a compelling case; you need to keep them engaged. Essentially, you need to lead them to what to think.

Your structure needs to change

It's crucial that you start to structure your presentations in ways that you might not have done in the past. Here are 10 things that are important to remember when creating a presentation for the digital age, no matter whether you deliver it virtually or in person.

ONE

Set a Clear Outcome

When you start to pull together slides without giving thought to what you want to have happen, you're going to make mistakes in your content. What do I want people to do or say after the presentation (in the context of what they do and say now)?

This shouldn't be surprising to most, but one of the most common pieces of feedback I get when training people is that this is one of the most important things they suddenly realise they need to do. Just about everything we do in business requires planning. When we put together a business plan, we need to understand where we are now and where we want to be. Same with a marketing plan, financial plan... anything, because planning shows us the gap between where we are and where we want to be.

From there, we work out the steps we need to take to make that happen. Presentations are no different.

Coming into work, I had to know where my office was and where I was starting from (my home). Having those two points, I could then put a plan in place to get here successfully.

It's the same with presentations: you need to start thinking about your presentation in terms of, "What do I want the audience to do or say?" Working towards an outcome, rather than just throwing together information without giving it much thought, is the first and most critical step in developing an engaging presentation.

A good presentation happens before you stand up to talk. The presentation's outcome, or objective, is the most critical part and its planning is where a good presentation starts. That's what determines everything that does or doesn't go in the presentation.

Getting the right content in the right order is critical and you need something through which to filter your information; that filter is your objective or outcome. When you're at that point of "Do I include it, or don't I include it?" ask yourself, "If I don't include this, will it interfere with me achieving my objective?"

If the answer is no, then don't put it in. No one's ever walked out of a presentation saying, "That was a great presentation. I wish they'd had more slides!"

More than one outcome is no outcome

When I talk to clients about the presentation objective, I'll ask, "What do you want people to do or say at the end of the presentation?"

They'll often say something along the lines of, "Well, I want them to know that I turn over $500 million, that I spend $22 million in R&D, we've got 762 employees," and so on, and so forth.

It may seem a harsh judgment, but: so what if they know that? It's not about what they know, as I will make very clear.

You need to have clarity about your outcome. I recommend you complete the sentence: "At the end of the presentation I want the audience to..." In less than 25 words (including those), you write what you want them to do or say. For example, at the end of the presentation I want the audience to:

> Progress us to the next stage in the RFP or

> Buy our product, or,

> Make an appointment to discuss their requirements detail.

Whichever is the most appropriate outcome to your presentation.

It's got to be achievable

Your outcome needs to be in the context of what's achievable. If it's a big presentation, and it's an RFP, or an RFQ, it's unlikely when you're doing your credentials pitch, that they're going to say, "Yes, I want to buy from you."

Your objective at that point is to get on the tender list, not to do a presentation as to why they should buy your products. As you progress through that RFP, or RFQ, that outcome is going to change along the way.

For example, if you get on the tender list with the first presentation, then you respond to the tender and you're invited to do a presentation around that, your objective should be to make it to the next stage.

It's not appropriate to have an objective that says, 'At the end of the presentation I want the audience to buy our product,' because it's not going to happen. Your outcome needs to be in context of where you are, what is the best possible outcome for the presentation that you're giving at that time.

Certainly, there are some cases where they might sign on the dotted line after the presentation. If that's the case, that's fine. But don't think that every presentation you do is about making that happen. It's not going to work for you; you're going to have the wrong call to action, you're going to have the wrong content, you're going to have the wrong structure around it.

Think and plan clearly for what you want to get out of your presentation. Once you've got your objective set, everything then gets determined from there.

TWO

Content is King, Structure is Queen

How you construct your presentation and the things included in it are critical to it being effective. This is your presentation's narrative. Your narrative is not your story, that comes later. A narrative determines what and when things are used in a presentation and your intent is to get people agreeing with you every step of the way, so that at the end, they have no choice but to do or say what you want them to do or say. That happens through content and structure.

Your audience needs to go on a journey from A to B to C. In a business presentation, you need to back that up with evidence.

Which brings up a key point about the content of a slide.

Why do you create a slide?

In our training programs, I'll often ask: "Why do you create a slide?" I have people in these training programs who might have been making presentations for 15 to 20 years. When I asked them this question, they stare at me blankly. They've been doing presentations for so long, and yet don't have any rules or guidelines along which to create a slide. Presentations are such a critical part of a person's career success and they haven't developed any guidelines on why they create the medium's main tool. Amazing.

You create a slide for one of two reasons: to deliver, or to offer evidence for a key message. That's all. That's a really important thing to remember, because your slides are very valuable. If you have too many, then they become worth less and less in direct proportion to the number of unnecessary ones you have. Go through an old deck (or a current one) and look at each slide and ask if it's delivering or evidencing a key message. This, of course, implies that you can identify the key message (but more on that later).

What are you doing there?

If you create a slide to deliver or provide evidence on a key message, what then is the speaker's job?

Their job is to provide context and meaning to that key message, or that evidence. They are there to provide the emotional connection between that key message and the audience. They can do this via stories, anecdotes, or a whole range of other tools.

When you understand the difference between the role of the speaker and the role of the slides, you start to see why having lots of content on your slide interferes with effective communication. When you can identify what you need to say and what the slides need to do, the job of building an effective presentation becomes much easier.

THREE

It's All About the Why

This is a really big one. Most presentations deal with 'the what', they think it's about knowing stuff, but it's not about 'knowing'.

What does that mean?

Many of the presentations that come across our desk goes straight into 'the what' we're doing. And that doesn't make a difference to people.

I can prove that. I'm sure that there's a percentage who have been on a diet or know people that have been on a diet. And I'll ask you this question: did any of those people not know what to do when it came to losing weight? I would suggest that most of them did, most people know how to lose weight. They need to cut down their food consumption, change the type of foods they eat, they need to exercise more, and consume fewer calories than are being used.

Sure, there are types of foods, protein versus carbohydrates and the like, and you can go down to the minutiae about that. But ultimately, it's not about knowing. Most presentations are all about the knowing. But if it's not about the knowing, what's it about?

It is about 'the why'. Why do you need to know this? Why is this important? It needs to be the why from the audience's perspective. They need to buy the why, before they buy your idea.

Rather than the 'how', the 'what', the 'who', the 'when', which are obviously important, you need to have the audience clear on *why* they should do something. If there are calls to action on what you're going to do, and how that's going to be of value to them, that needs to be in there. I can't stress enough the need to make sure that you deal with the why. There is so much change happening that the only way to create change, to have people buy your product, or stay with you, or have the board approve your project is driven by accepting the 'why'. It is the fundamental part missing for most presentations, and the more powerful the 'why', the more likely you're going to get what you seek.

The proof point of that is around dieting, giving up smoking or anything you want to say where people seek to change their lifestyle. What is it that makes the difference? Where is the power that has a person lose weight? Or give up smoking? Or that which has a company change strategy? Or has a company invest hundreds of millions of dollars with you rather than your competitors, or not do anything at all. It all happens with the why.

The more powerful that 'why', the more likely it is to happen. It's not unusual to see a new parent successfully give up smoking after years of failed attempts.

Why? Because they've just had a child.

Someone loses weight. Why? Because their doctor told them they were going to have a heart attack.

A friend of mine had been a smoker nearly all their life, they tried to give up numerous times, unsuccessfully. When they saw a doctor, the doctor told them they'd be on an oxygen bottle in two years unless they give up smoking, such was the degree of damage to their lungs.

This friend of mine walked out of there, threw away the cigarettes, and never smoked again, because 'the why' had changed. Up until that point, he thought, "Yeah, I'm pretty impervious, I'm not going to need to worry about that", but when they found out that they were going to get emphysema if they didn't stop smoking, suddenly, the 'why' had changed.

Make sure whenever you're putting a presentation together, that you've put the large amount of 'the why'.

It's easy to forget. I was writing something for a new service we've got coming out, putting together the promotional material about it. I gave it to my General Manager to read; she gave it back to me, pointing out I'd missed 'the why'.

It's something we can very easily do: omit 'the why'. Every point during the presentation needs to be highlighted with "Why this is important to what I'm telling you". The stronger you make 'the why', the more likely you are to make a difference. If you are going to get people to do what you want them to do by the end of the presentation, they need to buy 'the why'.

A couple years ago, I was in Singapore. As I was walking down the street, I saw this fabulous sign:

550 new buses are here with 450 more arriving. That's 'the what', and there is no engagement with that. If you can say 'So what?' to something, you have a problem with what you're saying.

OK, so I lied to you: that's not what the sign read. I work with a group of very talented designers. I got them to Photoshop this to remove the most powerful part of the message, the actual sign reads "550 new buses are here with 450

more arriving. So you get home sooner for play time."

Inclusion of that white text massively changes the context of why those 550 new buses and 450 more arriving are important. How often do you do that when you're giving a presentation? It's really important. When I saw this, I was so impressed with the power of its delivery of a data point, and why that's important.

What do you need to do?

You need to provide understanding, not a data dump. 'The why' creates the emotional connection; you achieve that through stories, case studies, anecdotes. The other important point to remember, so clearly pointed out by

John Medina in his fabulous book Brain Rules, is that the human brain cannot process information for more than 10 minutes straight.

It cannot just absorb data, data, data for more than 10 minutes; you need to give it an opportunity to assimilate that information. Give context and meaning around it. You do that with stories and case studies and anecdotes; it makes a big difference to giving an understanding and creating emotional engagement and memorability around the content in your presentation.

Make it personal

The more personal you can make 'the why', the more impact and influence it will have. Governments have been telling us for years that we should stop smoking. My friend only gave up when the implications of continuing were personal. It's the same when you are presenting. If you can weave personal appeal in there it will have far more effect.

Years ago, I was working with a client on a tender to be delivered to bank. It was a massive deal, so we went through everything we knew about the selection committee: their interests outside their direct responsibility in the process. For example, we identified one member who had a huge interest in 'big data'. Even though it wasn't part of his remit in the tender process, I made sure I included discussion of this in his section of the tender document.

FOUR

Slides Support Your Talk

When I train people, I ask them, "What's your role? What's the most important part of a presentation?" Very often they'll say, "The slides."

That's absolutely not the case. The most important part of your presentation is the actual person doing the presenting. It's their job to give the context and meaning to the information that's on the slide, which, of course, is a key message, or evidencing a key message.

What does this look like?

Imagine I gave a presentation and I had one slide and I said, "You are great". I spoke for 20 minutes with the "You are great" slide. People would, hopefully, walk away from that presentation with an understanding that they're... great.

That's good. So I think, "I'm doing this really well, people are really getting my message, I'm going to introduce another slide."

The next slide I introduced is "You're fast". You're great at what you do, and you're fast at it as well.

I have a 20-minute presentation that has two slides in it, telling your brain "You're fast", and I'm assuming that people get that message. I start to think I'm good at this, I've got this presentation thing handled.

Thinking that, I decide I'm going to use another slide, "You're cheap" (not meaning that in a rude way). So now I'm telling my audience "You're great, you're fast, and you're cheap."

And then I introduce another one, "You're green, you're environmentally conscious."

What's starting to happen? With each slide, the key message of the previous slide is starting to lose its impact. The slides are really valuable tools: they're the things that deliver your key messages. You need to be very careful with them, you don't want too many of them. Do that and you get information overload and people can't remember everything you've got on it (no, you DON'T need a slide when you ask them to turn off their mobile phones).

Do your slides work? Do they work as a basis to support what you're saying? Your job, your context and meaning to the key message is creating emotional engagement with the material and talking to people... not just reading from the slides.

The biggest single complaint we find in all our research is a lack of engagement coming from presenters simply reading from slides as they give their presentations.

FIVE

Make Your Proposition, Then Prove It

Tell a story, they say... easier said than done though. What does that mean, to tell a story?

In the era of virtual meetings and digital presentations, telling a story is essential to keeping your audience engaged, but the concept of creating a story frightens or confuses many presenters. It's actually quite simple, but like anything, only if you know how.

Without going into the structure of a story, I'll make it simple: we create stories every day in our conversations with people, which is exactly that we need to do in a presentation. The difference is, in a presentation, we are going to bring a structure to it that we may not be conscious of in our daily conversations.

Firstly, make you presentation title a proposition or a statement (this should, of course, be somehow related to your presentation objective). A proposition is simply what you aim to put out there with your presentation.

This crystalises two things: where the audience is now about that statement/proposition and where they should be at the end of your presentation. With a starting point and an end point, I have the essence of a story... and that story will take the audience from the former to the latter.

You do this with just about every conversation you have in daily life except the proposition usually goes unsaid, and often assumed, depending upon the relationship you have with the person you are talking to. A presentation varies from a story insofar as it is a structured conversation, with a clearly defined objective. Like a conversation, and unlike a speech, it is intended to be two way, its essence is engagement through that conversation, rather than being didactic.

Consider this: if your presentation title just says, "Range review", what room do you have to tell a story here? However, if it said, "How to disrupt the category and make more money for XYZ", you have now set the scene to be able to tell a story. You will also have piqued the interest of the audience. If you are in the audience, and you work for XYZ, at the very least, the thought arises, "Well, this will be interesting".

Delivering bad news? Rather than just saying "May 2020 profit forecast", try "Why we won't have reached projected profits by May 2020". These give you so much more to work with as a presenter and the audience will be listening for that storyline.

SIX

Use Your Titles to Deliver Your Key Messages and Tell Your Story

I was once talking to a client about a presentation his company had supplied him. The company sold voice recognition software for use by phone systems. Hidden deep inside slide 16, was a case study result, in 10-point type, two thirds down the slide, 3rd bullet point in the paragraph containing this fact: In XYZ company, our product reduced incorrect redirection of 44 million customers' phone queries in the course of a year by 11.2%.

That is nearly 5 million mistakes prevented... 3,500 per day, 562.5 every hour... nearly 10 every second. All in 10-point type! This should have been shouted from the rooftops, not buried in 10-point type!

In this age of our audience being bombarded by messages, it is absolutely essential that we identify our key messages and make them loud and clear. The best place for that is in the slide title.

Our slide titles should tell the audience the things we want them to remember when the presentation is over, the things we hope they will discuss over coffee when we've left the room or, these days, when they have stopped staring at the screen. It amazes me how many people waste this most valuable piece of screen real estate.

I very often seen slide titles that simply say, "Market Share" or "Sales Results". Your slide title should tell us what is happening with "Market Share" or "Sales Results", because they form the reason for your presentation so say what's happening right at the start. In this world of busy people, people who don't have time to waste, you need to make it easy for them to get the key message. Tell them what they need to know about market share: "Market share rose 2.3% in the July quarter" or "Sales results were below budget in the first three months".

Take the associated illustration as a further example.

A Slide Title that just says "Where we operate" says nothing of value because it's all about you, the presenter. Even if they were to remember that after your presentation, there is no message for them. If we changed that title to "We can serve your offices worldwide" has a far greater impact! When they remember that, they remember your key message and what it means.

If you don't feel you have anything to say, or that it's not your place to make

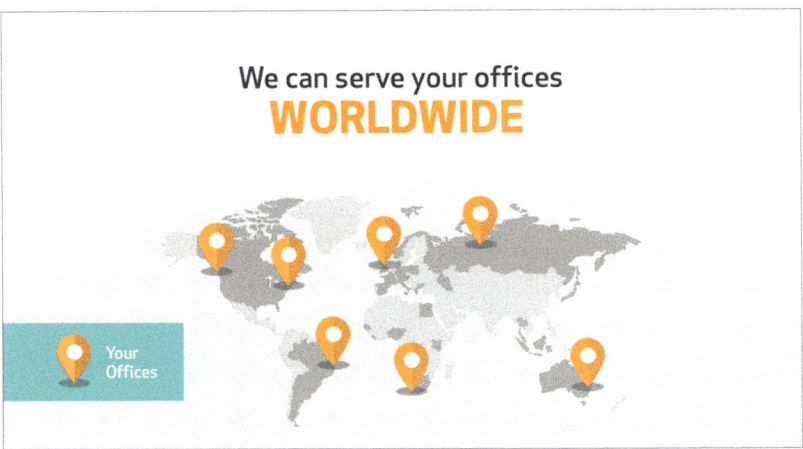

those judgment calls, then maybe you should not include the slide or, in the case of the latter point, maybe you shouldn't be doing the presentation at all!

The slide's title is like the headline of the newspaper: it's there to grab attention and deliver the key piece of information, hopefully inspiring the audience to read on. The newspaper headline grabs people's attention, and the body copy provides evidence and expands upon the headline. Even if they don't read further, they will have gleaned some message from the headline. It's the same with your presentation: deliver the message in the title and prove it (if necessary) with the content.

The title should deliver your key message of the slide: the content should provide evidence for it.

Once, when training a VP for Communications for a very large multinational, they pointed out they will spend hours trying to work out the title for their social media article because they know how important it is, but barely spend a second thinking about a slide title.

In your digital presentation, people are easily distracted, so you need to slam down that message as soon as the slide comes up. The content is only necessary to offer evidence or prove that point.

Now, tell your story

A presentation is just a conversation, and it's the slide titles that do that as well.

Imagine you're having coffee with a friend and told them you're giving a presentation called: "How to disrupt the category and make more money for XYZ".

"Oh", they say, "Tell me how."

You would start by laying the groundwork in the current situation, its background, then what you did, what happened and why, followed by a conclusion. You may, if necessary, bring out a chart or table to show them something you can't easily explain.

Construct your presentation in the same way.

Imagine, when telling your friend you only had 20 or 30 sentences to tell this story. You'd construct the story very carefully, thinking about what they needed to know to understand and follow you, making sure every sentence mattered and delivered a key point. These sentences are the titles to your slides, written just like you would say them to your friend (although you should keep them tight; no long sentences here, please. Two lines maximum).

In fact, you should be able to read your slide titles as sentences to a colleague, and at the end, you should have proved your proposition to them. They should have been able to follow your logic, understand your meaning and hopefully, agree with your proposition. If you can do that, you have constructed a perfect presentation.

The role of slide content

It is, despite any doubts you may have, really that easy. What about all the slide content? What about all the hours I've spent collecting all the information, don't I need it?

Your content exists just to give evidence backing up that point. That's all, nothing more, nothing less. There's no mystery in that, is there?

If you have a chart, the chart should prove the point you made in the title. I should only need to look at the content if I don't believe or understand the slide title.

Oh, and one more thing...

If you are required to send out your presentation to attendees as a pre-read, they will love you for this; it makes pre-reading easy as they can just read the headings and only look at the content if they need proof. No longer will they need to plough through your slides to see your point.

SEVEN

Be Animated

When I first started using PowerPoint back in 1997, they had an option on any of the animations, whether it be a transition, or an animation itself, in a function called 'Random'. I can only assume it was put together by a programmer who had no insight as to how to present.

You could put this random effect in, and anything could turn up. You get bouncy things coming into the slide, and things swirling and spinning. This is the common mistake I see in any new technology: the technology itself becomes what is important, rather than the technology's purpose.

It's interesting when we're talking about virtual reality and augmented reality: these are certainly going to make a difference in the way we communicate. One of the problems that we face is that as that technology becomes generally available, we have to make sure that the technology doesn't become entertainment; that the focus is still on successful delivery of the message, whatever that message is.

However, the outcome of having this 'Random' option in PowerPoint was that people stopped animating after their audiences got sick of the swirling and bouncing.

It was the same with the ability to put in sound. I used to lecture and of course, if you've been to university, you know you must do presentations as part of your assessment criteria in most units. If I had $1 for every student who put some clapping or applause at the end of the presentation, assuming that they were the first person to do so, I'd be sitting on an island somewhere where it was nice and warm, sipping an exotic cocktail with a small umbrella in it.

Why should I animate?

Your job as a speaker is to manage what the audience thinks about and what the audience is focusing on.

If everything is on one slide I guarantee that the audience reads the content on a screen before the presenter speaks to them about it. That happens with everybody. If I want to manage you through a presentation, then I should limit the options of what you can focus on. If I don't, while I'm talking to you about 'Subject X', you're reading the part about 'Subject Y'.

We use the same part of the brain to read as we do to listen. If I'm reading, I can't listen, so there's a good chance you're not going to hear what I say.

It's very difficult at that point to have people focus on what you as the speaker need them to focus on. You need to animate, but don't animate for entertainment value. You animate purely and simply to support your narrative.

What does that look like?

Let's imagine my 'Great' presentation mentioned earlier. I told people that they're great, and my evidence for that is because they're punctual, they're effective, they're unorthodox, and they're paradoxical.

Now I want to talk to you about why you're great, because you're punctual and how you're punctual and how that makes you great. All that other stuff ... but you're sitting there thinking, "What does he mean by paradoxical?"

I don't want you to do that; I want you to stay with me and talk about being punctual. So, I need to get rid of everything else and say, "You're great, because you're punctual." And then I can tell you all the reasons why.

Then I can take you to 'You're effective' and tell you why being effective makes you great, and so on. And then 'Unorthodox', and finally get to 'Paradoxical'.

Maybe I can bring all of those up at the end, to give you all the reasons that you are great. People will read what you put up on the screen when you put it up there, that's a guarantee. If you put it all up there at once, they're not going to listen to you.

If you put a lot of text on there, a couple of things will happen: if you are the presenter, and you have a lot of text, it's very hard not to read what's up there. Very often, that just leaves you with nothing left to say, and you can't add anything to it.

Secondly, when you read to people, they can read a lot faster than you can read to them. They've finished it while you're halfway through narrating it. You're not adding anything.

You need to make sure that you animate to support the narrative. I don't animate for 'whiz bang' reasons. That's just not the way to do it. It's just it's a step-by-step process to help you tell the story.

What about bandwidth?

In this digital age, it is appropriate to ask if animations are still necessary. After all, it takes extra bandwidth and that can cause problems.

In part, this is true; animations certainly used to cause problems. In a business context it's less of a problem, for two reasons:

1. Most business have access to high speed Internet capable of handling video.

2. The client/server relationship has been dramatically improved by software vendors over recent years, so it is far more bandwidth friendly.

Having said that, it is something of which we should still be conscious. If you are just doing a screen share it's not as big a problem than if you are broadcasting from within an app. For example, inside of Microsoft Teams, you can play a presentation directly from the app, rather than screen sharing. This doesn't seem to support some of the more complex animations like morph and some fonts don't appear correctly. Always test, test and test again before you do anything.

EIGHT

Start Big, Become Small

A lot of people go into too much detail, too quickly. The audience doesn't understand the context of what being talked about, so they don't get your message. When they don't get your message, they're more likely to say no to whatever you are suggesting—because people naturally avoid risk.

Providing this context can happen in several ways.

Use an Agenda

One best way to avoid these things is through crafting agendas. If you have a presentation going longer than 20 minutes, and isn't self-explanatory in its process, you should use an agenda, to which you should refer back whenever you move from one agenda point to another.

If your presentation says the 10 best ways to kill a mockingbird, you don't necessarily need to put an agenda in place, as you're aware which number you're at as you progress towards 10.

One key thing to remember is that your agenda should not be more than six points. Some agendas look like a table of contents. There must have been 20 or 30 different levels, 20 or 30 different points in it. Things like that just overwhelm. All we're trying to do is tell a story, outline that story to people, and foreshadow what we're going to cover.

A very basic agenda, comprising of a maximum of six points takes the audience through what they need to know and what you're going to cover on the day. They will be terrified if you bring up an agenda that has 12 points, trust me!

Explain the complex with a context

In the area of complex systems and processes, too often people have something they want to explain in terms of production processes, sales processes, any one of a number of things. They go into too much information, too much detail, too quickly.

Several years ago, a client who worked in the locomotive sector called us in to help them with a presentation. They showed us the slides and they said, "We're having trouble with people understanding where we actually add value, why we add value and why it works."

These were the slides he was showing us.

GRAIL 1

Grail 1 is an European Project that has involved **Signaling Systems Providers (ASTS, Alstom, Siemens, Bombardier, Thales), GPS System Providers (Thales Alenia Space, others)**, Consultants and Railway Organizations for three years. It ended in July 2008.

The main achievements of GRAIL 1 are:
- GNSS subsystem high level specification set (agreed by users and industry) for:
  - ERTMS/ETCS Enhanced Odometry application
  - Enhanced ERTMS/ETCS applications (Absolute Positioning, Train Awakening, Cold Movement & Train Integrity)
- Development and preliminary testing of a prototype of the GNSS subsystem for the Enhanced Odometry in both a real ERTMS/ETCS line and a lab environment, to draw conclusions concerning the mentioned specification,
- A preliminary Safety Analysis of the GNSS related applications,
- A preliminary Cost/Benefits analysis,
- A preliminary study on Local Elements augmentation systems.

Ansaldo STS provided the On Board Subsystem and Thales Alenia provided the GPS interface for the prototype

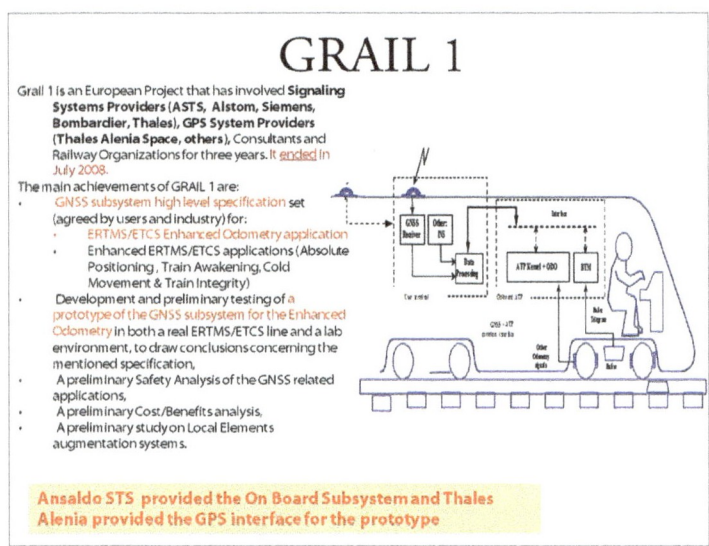

Alaska Rail Road Corporation (ARRC)- Collision Avoidance System (CAS) Architecture

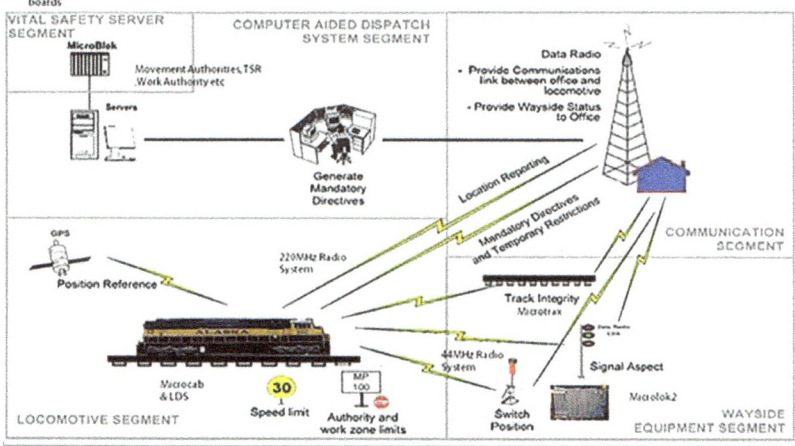

Looking at them, you can understand why people couldn't quite understand what the whole process was. We took a step back and tried to figure out what the audience needed to understand in this case: what exactly was happening.

We simplified one of their slides to be like the next few slides, providing far more context to the original purpose. As this was animated; they stepped us through it, explained what happened, and the role of everything.

When they were done, they brought up the locomotive and started to speak about how that technology interfaced with what happened in the railway system, how that made a difference, and so on.

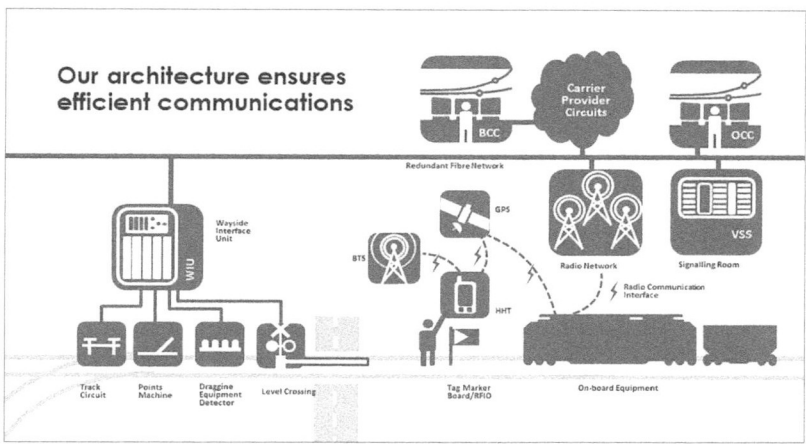

NINE

Keep Slide Content to a Minimum

Everybody knows that we need to keep slide content to a minimum, yet presentations continually have huge amounts of data in them, with complex tables and lots of text.

Why? As we have already seen, 'Knowing' something doesn't make any real difference; you need to understand why it's important. There's a gentleman named Edward Tufte – professor emeritus of political science, statistics, and computer science at Yale University. Generally recognised worldwide as the thought leader around the delivery of statistical information, he has published some great books. (If you're ever at a loose end, you could read those books, you'll find that they're not as bad as they sound).

He has a philosophy regarding statistics and delivery of data, particularly with regards to charts, where he has what he calls a 'data to ink ratio'. The data to ink ratio says you should only have sufficient data on a chart to deliver the information. No more, no less. If you add any more ink on that chart, you won't improve the understanding of the information.

Or if you take any away, you will make it less effective. A one-to-one ratio is ideal.

When I read this, I thought this same thing applies to presentations. If I use the metaphor of ink in the context of a slide, I can develop what I call an 'info to ink ratio'.

Every slide in a presentation must have a reason for its existence. The reason for its existence is to deliver or provide evidence for a key message.

What does that mean?

The first thing that you should do is take your logo off every slide.

Our area of vision is about the same as a thumbnail at arm's length; that's the area we can focus on when looking at something. All the rest of it is purely for peripheral vision. Peripheral vision is good at noticing change, but it's really bad at noticing detail.

We stop seeing things that are the same, and that is physiologically programmed into us. Peripheral vision is there to notice change, because 'change' might present opportunities or threats to us. It's a part of our evolution.

Why is this important? If you have the logo in the same spot in every slide, we just stop seeing it. But how often have you had to compromise the information that you put on a slide – a chart, a table, a complex process flow – where you've had to put it below the title and above the logo and it ends up too small to read.

The decision making is quite clear around this: if something on the slide doesn't help with the delivery of the information, get rid of it.

But don't forget to brand

That doesn't mean you shouldn't brand; branding is essential. That's deeply built into marketing DNA. I'm a 'brand demon' when it comes to presentations, but it's a lot more than just having a logo on every slide.

What it does mean is that you need to think judiciously about how and where you put logos. I'd recommend only showing it on title slides and section headers, and occasionally, throughout the deck where it works.

To be effective as a presenter, two things are absolutely important. The first one is, you must make sure that people understand what you're saying. So that gets back to messaging, structure and engagement.

The second is they must remember who said it. Years ago, I was sitting at the Australian Stock Exchange, listening to CEOs present to a group of investors about why they should invest in their company. These were short presentations, of about eight minutes in length. There were six presenters during lunchtime, and all these CEOs stood up and said basically the same thing. They started with a share registry, the money in the bank, blah, blah, blah.

At the end of that series, it was difficult to remember who said what; this is where branding becomes important. This is where making sure that you are delivering what the people need to hear to make that decision, and that you are doing it in a way that is memorable, so they can remember who said what.

Marketers will tell me, "I can't take the logo off my slides, because that's my brand". If you're so serious about the brand, do you have the responsibility to determine who presents? Some people are bad presenters. They do not do your brand any good by presenting.

Think clearly about the 'info to ink ratio'. I only ever have on my slides the things that are important. Maybe take the load off, if necessary, so you have key points and justification and evidence on the slide.

TEN

No Third Level Bullet Points

The quickest way to end someone's involvement in any presentation, particularly a digital or virtual one, is to drown them in text. We all know this but still people do it. They do it for a couple of reasons:

1. They forget that a presentation consists of a speaker and slides and they think that they need to put all the information on the slide. As a result, they, the speakers, become redundant. When you put lots of text on a slide, as a presenter, you can't help but read it. Yet, the audience can read it faster than you so they just end up waiting for you to finish and there would be nothing left to say, so you roll on to the next slide and do the same thing. Meanwhile, all those people who are watching it on their computers have started reading their emails, or making phone calls.

2. They don't have confidence in themselves and don't understand the way presentations work so feel the overwhelming need to put every detail on the slide.

You see, many people think that the detail is important in a presentation and while there are some cases for it, mainly there isn't.

Presentations are not good for teaching and or learning detail or, to use the Latin, learning things verbatim: word for word. If you need to commit something to memory, few people can do that in a traditional presentation situation. This usually requires you to go away and recite, recite, recite until you commit it in memory. This is also something we tend to do alone.

Not much thought is given to what people need to see around presentation material. People don't need to remember the detail, to be able to quote it after the presentation, they just need to understand what is being said at the time.

Presentations don't work well for detail, but they excel at giving an overview, or gist, of an idea, concept or proposal. That, in combination with the speaker, means there is seldom a reason to go to third level bullet points for a presentation. It is a level of detail that is just not necessary in a presentation.

I make the last point there purposefully. Some managers want the details, right down to the very nitty gritty. If so, it's best to give this as a leave behind, rather than the presentation itself. Their beliefs aren't supported by any research around presentations but on odd occasions these people are in positions of influence around some organisations and their vanity needs to be catered to.

And now...

That's your presentation. Simple enough when you know how.

You are now unique. Most people haven't even read a book like this one on presenting, they are simply doing what they have always done, unthinkingly, so well done on finding out how to do it better.

This won't be an easy change for you. I've trained in this long enough to think it will be easy. You will strike resistance in several areas, more than likely from those further up the organisational ladder. One hallmark for some senior managers is they think they are great presenters (the degree to which they think that is usually inversely proportional to their staff who think the same) but hang in there, if you can. Give them this book to read if you wish.

Also, like anything, you will need to practise it and internalise what you have read. That will take time. Like anything new you try, it won't flow like your current way of doing things flows because you will need to break ingrained habits.

Good luck and great presenting! Remember, it's not what you say that is important, it's what they take away!

Acknowledgments

A special thanks to several people. Firstly, the guys at The Big Smoke for getting me to do this, particularly Matt Reddin who did a lot of the initial work and editing.

Secondly, Sandy, my partner, who I woke up (unintentionally) every morning at 5.00am to get to the office so I could get the space to do this. Writing doesn't come easily to me, it's like drawing blood sometimes, so her support around this and every other area of my life is just phenomenal. I certainly wouldn't be where I am without her support and I scratch my head constantly wondering how I was lucky enough to find her.

Thirdly, my wonderful staff. What an inspirational group of people to work with. You teach me new things every day, present me with new challenges and supply me with the privilege to lead you. I will be eternally grateful and look forward to what we will create with PowerfulPoints.

Thank you, Lynne Hendrick who suggested I do this, as a business; neither of us thought it would look like it does today. One passing comment and look what happened, we should never underestimate the power of what we say.

Finally, to all our clients. Thank you for the opportunities to work with you and be able to draw on the experience and insight that has allowed me to access.

Lightning Source UK Ltd.
Milton Keynes UK
UKHW021834201121
394260UK00006B/232